NOW NEVER STOPS

ANON EDITION

2020
Flagstaff   West Palm Beach   Los Angeles

NOW NEVER STOPS

C. Brooke Rothwell

Illustrations by

Byron Baker

Edited and designed by Thom Burns
First issued as a private printing in 2019 as *Poems*
ISBN: 978-1-71673-298-0

For Elora and Kabelo

1

The blood motor explodes

Caught on film in the old Paramount Theater

Swarming with pollen and the puissance of stars

Wine pours pure as midnight

Waiting for paint to peel

'

The mystery of reflection

Reconstructs the kinetic life of an atom

Laughter is the lifespan of a cloud through a room

Left to their own devises

The drone of Tibetan baritones becomes the glue

Of wanted posters

While buffoons kick the gong around

The centerpiece blooms accordingly

On behalf of a full moon

For breakfast

Ectoplasm handprints on the Eucharist

Intensify the silence of empty bowls

Placed along the highway of Neptune

5

Cast aside your foibles

Rendering the riveted iron mask rudderless

Deliver unto the dirigibles their discarded toothpicks

Remember all saints are normal but without navels

Just as the pyramids of Mexico are upside down

When standing on one's head

On the heart altar

Squeeze the vocabulary of synthesis

Feel the symbols ooze synonyms of coincidence

The moment of death is a possible moment

If you feel separate then go back

And try again to experience your One Self

I urge you to daydream as often as you can

You'll be taking a giant step forward

Dust will not follow you

And the buttons on your spats will sparkle

Paracelsus and his alligators

Traipse the hills and valleys

Searching for the impossible rose

But bliss is not a passive state

Ask the alchemist

When he's not too busy

Pruning his roses

Cast not your slippers before the fate of Isis

Lest the bloodthirsty temple priests

Discover your trailblazing ways

Hidden among the reeds like baby Moses

Waiting for the scarlet ibis of el-Amarna

To lead you on the trail of the mummy trade

To the crypt of madness

With music by Harpo Marx

Heart throbs in the ambrosia of the air

Empires brought low by mere messenger pigeons

My ambitious game backfired

Against and over the orchestra pit

Don't reach out for me

I'm drowning too

Down the mouth

Of a tuba

Auction the latest undertows on any street corner

Tiger-headed carpets cruises the aroma of a nocturne

While the brass toes of idols are polished

By street urchins

Smoking Sweet Caporals

The sea is rising

Rainforests are burning

Birds are disappearing

Humans ride their goats nonchalantly

To the altar of slaughter

The earth composes a bill of revenge

Delivered on a tombstone

To a corner of the Milky Way

13

Meanwhile down by the river

Water leaps to the rescue of her reflection

Men cannot memorize her eyes

My sex is pollinated

By her glance

Opposites become kingdoms when rubbed together

Moss haunts the eyes of a statue

Sages sleep the sleep of *The Boy who Flew*

But remember hieroglyphics cannot be read this way

15

While television is being overthrown

Witness the majestic death throes

Of the king in overalls

16

Osiris high on rutabagas

Starry-eyed starlets adorn the ceiling

Lucky snake charmers with immaculate eyelashes

Sound the alarm

On a wall

Sweating pitch

17

Cherries of swans

Preened by the air

Bask on the drift of love

Eyes caressed by their lids

18

Fainted woman in my arms

Neck vulnerable as space surrounding a blade

Beneath her lids nothing but the scanning of REM

And me on the high seas

Scaling the Sphinx

In full arousal

19

The emerald eyes of an alligator

Stir not the sparkle of a star

With its omnipotent patience

Of deaf teeth

People enjoy getting cremated

While tombstones sentinel sentimental hieroglyphics

Ashes have no memory of ashes

Only the lifespan of flames

And cremation has a longer shelf life

With no expiration date

Place your top hat over the drumbeat of a Victorian rug

Situate the glimmer of candlelight on her lacquered lips

Now consecrate the dreamer of the berserk

On the altar of outer space

Life having no opposite *

In Egg Land

Here at evolutions' end-of-the-line

My sign breaks free of the zodiac

Merging between the eyes of an egg

As seen from the interior

23

I'm in love with a girl with brown bangs

For me she streamlines the castles' passageway

Phosphors glow of midnight exits the window

She should have been home hours ago

But we kept entering and re-entering the castle

As I said

I'm in love with the girl with brown bangs

24

Peacock of dawn

Disguised as a millinery's dummy head

Laughs behind a newspaper

Waiting for a train

Which is sunrise

Always on time

The fountain of youth

Spouts flames

Some people are petrified of the forest

Life is like that

Before the weightless victory

Of the veracity of fire

At large

26

Who knows the whereabouts of the black butterflies of the grotto

Their silence breeds the violence of silence

Meanwhile your feet are a million years old as youth

Toes beautiful as fingers

With joints of quicksilver

And honeydew

Finally I can fondle the clouds

With you holding hands

Laughing at the man whose head looks like an engine

In profile

Tying each other up in forget-me-nots

And fleur-de-lis

28

You're a pupil of the moon

I'm the opposite of numbers in a trance

Balanced on ice needles

Damselflies demystify wind chimes

Oscillating the velocity of love's irresistibility

Spinning inside-out

In the palm of my hand

29

The stampede of stars on parade

Bloodlines speed through fire alarms

Uniting the clocks

Of all time

30

Don't stop now

Now never stops

Its round head

Exploding in slow motion

The way galaxies imitate shredded Ferris wheels

31

Consciousness speaks only to consciousness

This explanation may inspire you

When planning your next move

As your heart beats in a determined relationship

With a bittersweet

And revelatory counterpoint

The ancient custom of crossing femurs

Under a skull

Recalls the pendulum

Without a fixed point

Fireflies seethe around the Philosopher's Stone

The end desired from the beginning

33

On the balcony of a space ship

Man plays a fiddle

His leotards shredded by radiation

He holds the earth in perspective between two fingers

Behind his mask of gravity

He somersaults in holy meditation

The space station a sarcophagus

Where babies on their way to Mars

Play monopoly

With real money

34

The origin of matter

That is the question

Is it not?

35

Mirabilis at midnight

The eye of Nefertiti

Left on a ballroom floor

Maidens line up to see if it fits

Chopin plays his dirge in the background

Don't disturb the cow

Under the piano

36

Nurtured in the fetal genesis of light

I thought I had to search beyond you

For keys to the wind

I didn't see the eggs of opposites

Between your hips

I just didn't see your vastness

Obvious as the sea

37

Contrary to handmade prophesies

Nothing in this room makes sense

Except you

Lit up by your Hermetic correspondences

You with your science of symbols

Rippling to the rhythm

Of celestial mathematics

38

God's girlfriend

Pirouettes atop a tree stump

Fairies curtsey like dimples on her fingertips

God grins like a knucklehead

Placing a juicy fruit between her lips

39

Cause frolics with the illuminati

Spinning on its one toe upon the fulcrum of all effects

Buried up to its eyeballs in ticker-tape

Let's trim the spider's goatee

40

Egypt holds me in its hands of everlasting dust

I run my fingers through the hair of sands' transparency

In the end

Time is one long now

Top hat left in a tree

At the end of a gothic novel

Now fetch Yin and Yang

From the back room

42

I watched the Arctic catch fire

While nature's night watchman dozed

Ribbons of golden afternoons streamed from the eyes

Of rootless children

Whales beached themselves

Before the fireplace

But it was only a dream

43

Imagine the voyage of the messenger

If this quest still beckons

Consider the parallel between cabbage

And its offspring the bayonet

Among the many adventures

Of the open window

44

In the mirror of quintessence

The same cause

With different subjects

Gives similar effects

45

Hydras at the windows of the manor house

And who'll retrieve the fingerprints of the sun

To bear upon the spectacle

Of humanities captivating bloodbath

Drowning in celebrity

46

Bernadette Soubirous

Brews tar stimulating the Pope's senility

Original sin stalks the town of Lourdes

Balanced atop a fountain

Of puerile ideals

47

Doctor Solar

Found the idea of a bird

Rather too exceptional

To be realistic

48

'

Hidden in the aural rhapsodies of mescaline

A translation of intense lyricism

Copulates broadside with the

Origin of images

49

Roiling with life

Drowning in meaning

Speaking in spores

Unseen inhabitants

In the greenwood magic

Boil their own

Tears of nutrition

50

Gorging on a glut of light

Otherness releases the verb of eagles

On a different planet

Fossils in a trance

Polish the gift of seeing

51

Cold-hearted clocks

Incubate pre-natal aspirations

Born of the speed of anarchy shuffling its cards

Blood makes a U-turn

In the Parliamentary heyday of

Table tapping

52

Simulations of deliria

Delivered to the doorstep of springtime's spermatozoon

Brings out the best

Of the maniac's multicolored profundity

Frozen in drag

53

Longing for the fabled lips of Fatima

Visionary topography beckons

Mundus imaginalis provides but a glimpse of

Her body symbolic

Of the symbol itself

Beyond desire

But attainable through the essence of

Desire itself

54

Arrows carved from bird songs

Pierce the curl of a wave

By the light of the moon in a lantern

Mermaids

Switch on their sex eyes

Through venetian blinds

55

Children are the fingerprints

Of animated stars

Plotting the overthrow of the reality principal

With giant footprints

And butterfly eyes

A thousand miles wide

On the playground of pretend

56

Be careful love

Since the world began eating itself

Carriage whips and rubber-tired hacks

Abandon themselves to the nuclear power of nudes

Fingering the culprit

Of all the time in the world

57

Because the air is round

The silence of speed can be defanged

Framed and hung like the folly of wallpaper

From the head of

A chip off the old block

58

Harbingers of sultans

Beating their brains out

For the benefit of

The yin and yang

Of Siamese twins

59

Your imitation of her yawn

Recognizes its worth

Of true solidarity

With the coagulating force of

Katydids cavorting through Leviticus

60

The monster from forever

Singing like a dragonfly stilled by its elegance

Seduces the ramparts with sirens

Laughing in parables

Of jasmine

61

A very pellucid and informed apiarian

And a cow with folded wings

Plunge from the heights of the Ace of Hearts

With no edges

Free-falling

Through the midst of things

62

A man on his last bed

Imagines wild horses running out of

Silver plumage

Defending the tail feathers of an egret

From exhausted prophecies

63

The circularity of nature

Defended by granulated time

Perfection's elegance is reflected

By its labors of shamelessness

The color of mirrors

64

Let's runaway to the West

Past the eonian wisdom of rocks

Beyond the sword point of regret

Of caves lit by torches

Blown out by our passing

It's the destination of the journey

They say

The journey *is* the destination

Remind the sages

Who we carry like letters of introduction

In our beaded satchels

65

Whatever happened to the color of shadows

Pressurized by face-to-face silhouettes

Dispersed by the lightness

Of your touch

66

From the Babylonian solar system

Crawl out the nighttime guests

Of the previous year

Lovelorn and still searching for their lanterns

Their Load Star

Blew out ten million light years ago

Sentinels of sorrow

Still in equilibrium

67

Clinging to the granoblastic fig tree of Hathor

Truth from whence the fruit falls

To its knees

Before the imagination

68

Bow ties on future Gilas

Gives life to change

As tomorrow's tomorrow

Is always today

69

I made love to Venus in a haystack

She recited the poetry I was using

Nesting birds in the rafters

Gave spontaneous birth to starlight

So treasured by Moai

And their Mona Lisa smiles

70

All the coffins have been lined up by dynasties

Lotus flowers on the dance floor are in full bloom

As are unsheathed breasts

To the tunes of Johnny Dodds in a pharaohs' wig

And so sway the flappers

In the papyrus

71

Man the starlight

Sinew the corsets

Brave the sea spray of translucent fragments

For the sake of the loveliness of the enigma

But don't stay long

If it's not in the bag

72

In the super-mind

Birds wearing masks of the first-formed

Arrowhead through the ancestry of the infinite

The Gods have used up their cell-phone minutes

Loneliness stands with the ancients

Shouldering the statuesque void

73

Sun dusted and opened like a book

You waiting for me

Paris is so lovely

We love each other just right

Inside the grand hallway

Lacquer the walls

With ardent gel

74

Nervous patter of abandoned hats

The Prodigal Son returns in a zoot suite

Celebrations cast a dim light of bonfires in the distance

This room couldn't be darker

Than midnight bottled and corked

Dogs consume the genitals of the Duke

What a night for dreaming

75

We timed it perfectly to a splatter

Kissing at the corner of Charleston and Tiger Rag

Clarinet muskets fire at the mirrored moon

Drumsticks shatter glass cymbals

The last piano note hits the bottom of a well

Let's light up a Lucky for an encore

76

O broad daylight of Arabian nights

You have nothing to fear

From planet X

Read your magazine

Think in heaps

Draw your next breath

From the bulrush

The Case of the Pilfered Planet by Lord Jat

Using a blink comparator

A serendipitously beautiful spectacle

Roughly the size and shape of a grand piano

Pluto's plutonium heartbeat

Fortunately continued at 36,400 miles per hour

Until dinner time

78

A Calvary captain's monocle with the profile

Of a woman engraved on the face of it

He hit the ground running

Not knowing he was already dead

Wasps gradually covered his eyes

His monocle carried away

By a brave raven

79

The butcher's daughter

Takes her delight

From spoon feeding the moon

While the sun

Hands on its hips

Laughs like a decapitated statue

From the balcony of a

Sunspot

80

The rose that unsettles the night

Becomes the memory of all color

What stars do poets return to for reincarnation

While the sun's stepson cavorts in autumn leaves

My mother lives on somewhere in space

81

White hair of the stream

Let's return to the confidence of eyes

Of the smell of sagebrush and earth

Not this spell cast by unhealed hearts

Banking on the brilliance

Of a summer dusk

On crutches

82

People get paid to copulate

But without the ecstasy of

Reciprocal joy

Writhing alone on an island

Of profound hunger

83

The wing of dawn holds out its palm

Boats float by themselves on this dawn

The local Argonauts get tangled in their ivory sails and iron nets

Women laugh at them from windows

Daylight dazzles the unfocused eyes of flapping fish

The abandoned piano on the open road

Means it's a good day

For pillars grazing in the courtyard

84

Owl in the fading torchlight

Horses of dawn plod home

Their armor dented by old age

And children's stones

85

On the Elysian Fields

Councils await the virgin forest of a breast

Blue veined and suckling

The genius of a new man

86

The intoxication of cyclones

Conjures up the style

Of naked jewels being stripped by a gale

Burnished for introspection

By the wind

In heat

87

A handful of veins play the harpsichord

Shivers take effect

Cadavers sit straight up

Once I was a little boy

Fascinated by a little girl

Anyone who knows me

Knows the rest

88

The heart of a tree

At high noon

The disheveled old poet

Once a premier orator

Now polishes coffins in the shade

This shade itself

Cut from the heart of a tree

89

Right through the middle of a song

Through a bird's eye

Adopted

By a kiss perfectly cultivated

Nesting in a bull's eye

The last outpost of desire

Feasts on women and men signaling to each other

Of their greatest need

Beyond what fingers point to

Beyond cataclysms in the shadow of lashes

Beyond the meaning of black morsels

Beyond the fatigue of pain

Beyond the needs

Of all earthly hunger

For wholeness

91

A crow's nest on a comet

Sights the horizon of good and bad

In infinities' museum

Dear hearts behind glass

Classic in the manner of

Obsolete telescopes

92

She laughed with no idea

Of the effect her teeth were having

On the boy's first sexual awakening

Of the accurate accusations

Of mad love

93

Portrait of sleep

In a nutshell

Eases up on the gas

Passing through

Precious stones

In bloom

94

The grand finale gave birth

To the enigma shimmering in bloody splendor

Its mouth open like a stubborn idea

The orchestra discards its surgical gloves

For whalebone toothpicks

And stovepipe hats

For an encore

95

The horizon of Hindu gargoyles

And the silk of their eyelids

Their diamond belt buckles of mutiny

Their unspeakable crimes spreading over the city walls

Teaching dog grammar

To future orphans

In speakeasies

96

The avant-garde

With nothing to do

Gets drunk on peeling plaster

Revolutionaries pitchfork their ass

But old solutions are hard to dislodge

Better to dust the periscope

Than perish in hypothetical

Refractions of musk

97

A gang of zebu

With arrows through their humps

Gallop over everything that exists

Even the azure

And into the arms of

Dying gravity

98

With a trombone for a birthmark

I entered the plaza

De Chirico's statue was there

Along with the flags flying backwards

I was careful not to get too excited

About the impossible silence of the place

I had returned to Paris at the time

After having had my front teeth knocked out

But full of the grandeur

Of pure adventure

My tongue returning obsessively

To the space

Vacant as the silence

Of the plaza

99

The Ojibwa tame the genius of mollusks through friendship

While defending the stillness of crystal

The hiss of clouds birdshot with desire

Secrete the birth of volcanoes

In the pleats of your handprint

100

Corn fed shadows stalk the King of Bavaria

Scarabs escape from his side pockets

His muse lurking in the echo of perfume

Cross-dressed in a blond tuxedo

Bellows from the black castle

Scaring the daylights out of daydreams

Who tame the velocity of billiard balls

Sharing side pockets

With the returning Scarabs

101

Taking the turn on two wheels

Charlie Chaplin throws away the steering wheel

The crooner with the axel greased moustache

Shoots himself at the finish line

The crowd goes nuts

102

Without a fish

The bell of the ball

Drops anchor at the brink of despair

Rescued by the Prince of Dragonflies

Both balanced on a cattail

Above the songs of what can be sung

Her laughter in a humidor

For connoisseurs

103

Splitting the ray of moonlight

Across the pupil of an eye

I cast the demons out of

The mouth of Ra

I made my bed of unwrinkled glass

With the help of

Prophetic outcasts

I loved you then

And can never die

With your lipstick

On my collar

104

The erotic pulse is fadeless

The geometry of a shadow traces the contour

Of the shadow of a rose

Boxed in cellophane and delivered

To a Balinese dancer

105

Here where Paul Eluard drops globules of glass

Into steaming water

Velocity itself fissures into the arms of

Tibetan temple bells announcing the entrance

Of high kicking

Chorus girls

106

Capture her heartbeat in a jar

Balance it atop an obelisk

Its capstone

Blazing from the center

Of my forehead

107

Female planets juice the eyes of space hawks

Your fingers drip with Kabbalistic numerology

Castaways eat their last crossword puzzle

While

The tongue of the sea

Laps at the gate left open

108

Rumors of the utopia of catastrophe

Whittle the unpronounceable

Back to the vernacular

Little Lord Fauntleroy recites his Heraclitus

Facing sea spray of diamonds disintegrating

In reverse

109

The table is set for Queen Hatshesut

This carafe of blood

Will be empty by noon

Galaxies coagulate the eyes of star eaters

The Pope's head lands in his spaghetti

A shepherd is pulled off stage by his own staff

Replaced by hundreds of Nietzsches

The end of this particular world

Went by like a house

By the side of the road

Victorian maidens parade the boardwalk

Their bustles

Full to bursting

With shark fins

And fireflies

111

A black hole is the perfect ending

To poems of articulate smoke and a spatter of nightingales

Burning through what time thought it was

Consuming especially the deluxe souvenirs

Of a lifetime